ONE PROUD PENNY

RANDY SIEGEL ★ SERGE BLOCH

A NEAL PORTER BOOK
ROARING BROOK PRESS
NEW YORK

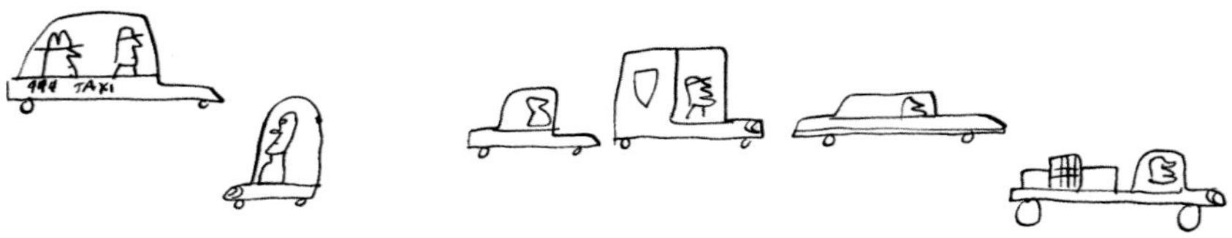
TAXI

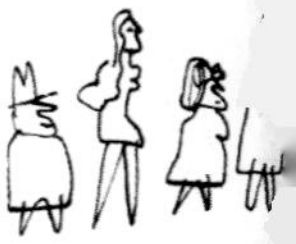

I was born in Philadelphia,
where the United States was born,

the home of

the Liberty Bell,

Patti LaBelle,

cream cheese,

cheese steaks,

soft pretzels,

and the United States Mint,

the place where most of our country's pennies are made.

I was born in 1983,

which makes me older than younger.

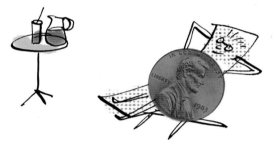

Most of us move around for twenty-five years or so before retiring,

but I'm still going strong,

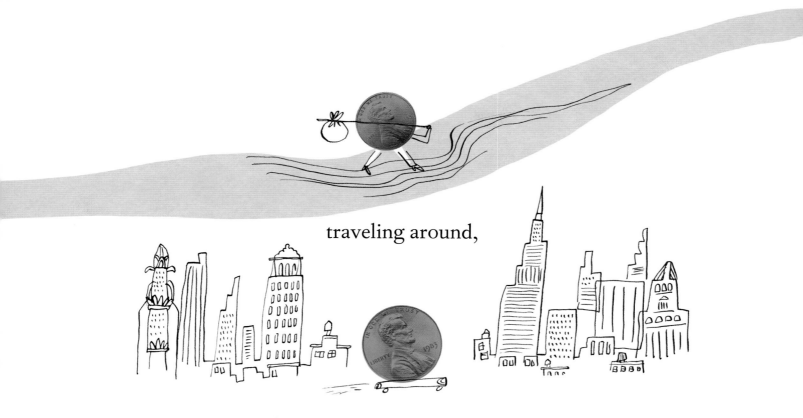

traveling around,

from state to state, city to city,

and pocket to pocket,

doing what I do best,
helping change the world.
Or to be more exact,
helping the world make change.

I am a penny.
A proud penny.
A single cent.
But there is nothing simple about me.
I'm one of 250 billion, if not more,
out there being passed around.

Not only can you spend me,

you can flip me,
toss me,

roll me,
spin me,

or pop me in a piggy bank.

During my life on Earth,
I've traveled from Philadelphia,

TO ALASKA

PACIFIC OCEAN

PORTLAND

UNITED STATES

LOS ANGELES

TO HAWAII

to New York, Los Angeles, Chicago,
Miami, Portland, Maine, and Portland, Oregon,
and most every place between,

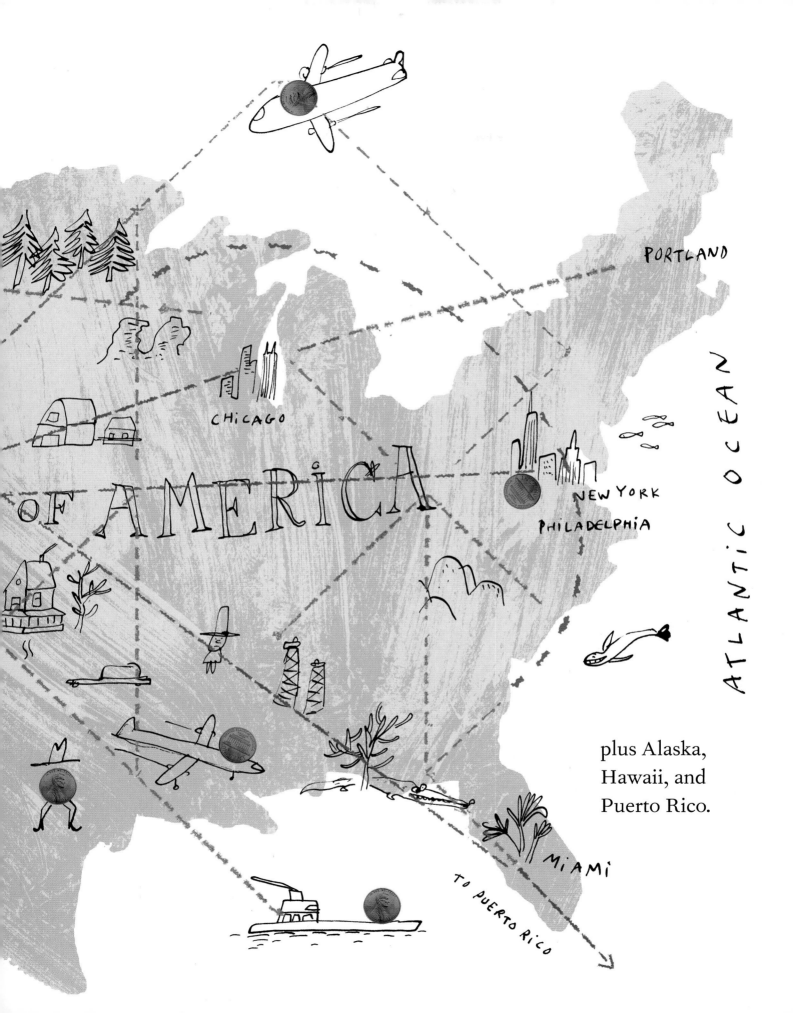

PORTLAND

CHICAGO

OF AMERICA

NEW YORK

PHILADELPHIA

ATLANTIC OCEAN

plus Alaska,
Hawaii, and
Puerto Rico.

MIAMI

TO PUERTO RICO

I survived one snowy winter,

freezing my tail off
on a garage floor in Green Bay, Wisconsin,

until I got picked up

and used to pay for
stuff several times,

before getting stuck underneath the stamp machine
in a post office near Pepper Pike, Ohio,
where I sat for three whole weeks.

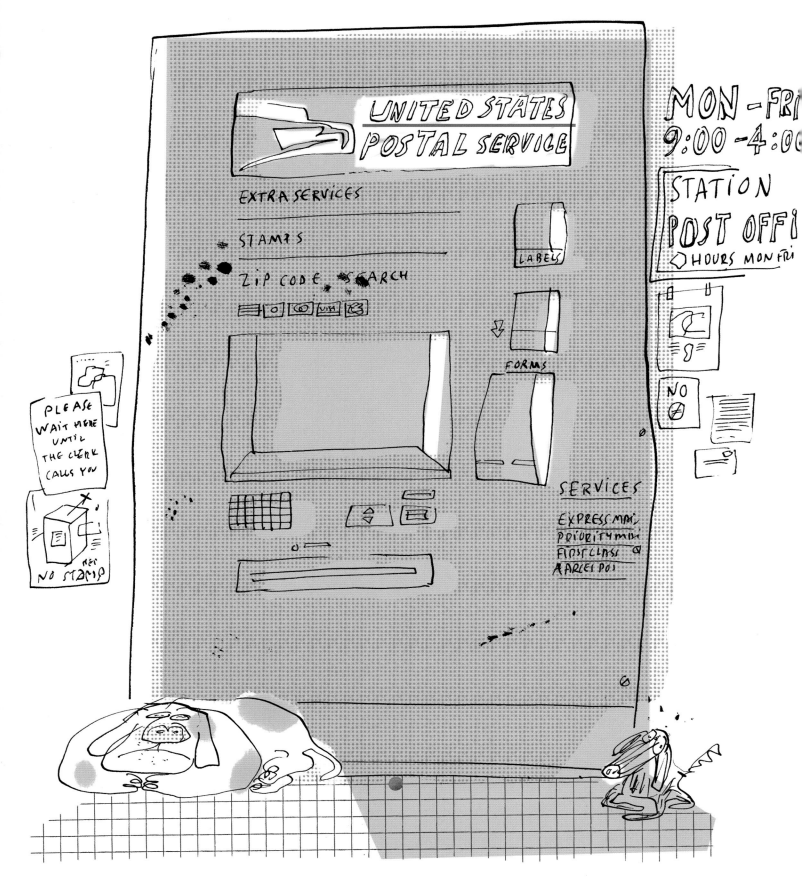

I hated being alone
and forgotten.

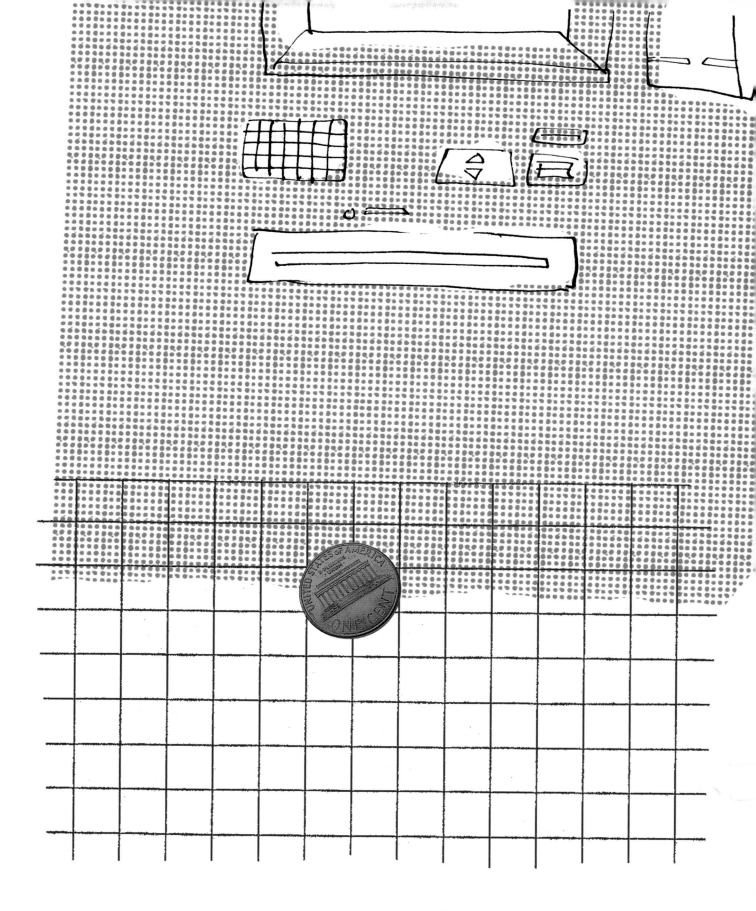

Who wouldn't?

Fortunately, some smart kid saw me on the floor,

snatched me up,

and took me to his house,

where I've been sitting ever since,
in their kitchen, on a counter, in a jar,

filled to the top with mostly pennies,
but also a few nickels, dimes, and quarters,
waiting patiently for whatever happens next.

In the past, I've been used to buy ice cream,

candy,

newspapers,

baseball cards,

super balls,

and a pair of purple polyester pants
at a JCPenney department store.

But I don't get much action anymore.
Most things in life have gotten more expensive,
while I remain just one red cent.

Some folks think pennies are worthless,
but I know we are worth a lot.
So what if we're not dollar bills?

We are stronger and better looking
than those green pieces of paper that
get wet, wrinkly, bent, and torn,
which we never do because we're
made out of metal.

Yes, pennies are 97.5 percent zinc and 2.5 percent copper.
In other words, I'm mostly zinc with a little copper,

unlike my parents who were mostly copper with a little zinc,

and my grandparents, who were bronze,
which means mostly copper with a little tin and zinc,

and my great-uncle who was gray
because he was born in 1943 and made out of steel,

like Superman.

I've lived a pretty good life,
but it hasn't been perfect.
I've been dropped, nicked, knocked, kicked, and scratched,

which is why I don't look anything like I did

when I was brand-spanking new,
as sparkling as the ocean on a bright, sunny day.

While I'm pretty happy most of the time,
I've had my fair share of problems.

I've been sucked up and stuck
in a vacuum cleaner more times than I can count.

I've bounced around more
laundry machines and dryers than I care to remember.

I once spent a year
in a sewer drain on the side of a busy street.

But I always manage to find my way out
of whatever jam I'm in,
because I am one tough penny.

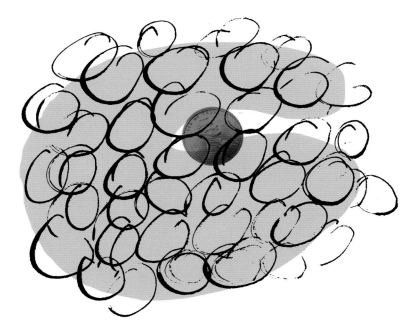

As I lie here in this jam-packed jar,
I try my best to be patient
and relax.

I think about Lincoln.
You know, Abraham Lincoln
(you can call him "Abe"),
whom I believe was the best U.S. president ever.

His face is on my front,
his memorial is on my back.

As my man Lincoln once said:
"Whatever you are, be a good one."
Which is the law I live by,

so I try to be the best penny I can.

Whoops! Sorry, I gotta go,
I just got grabbed.

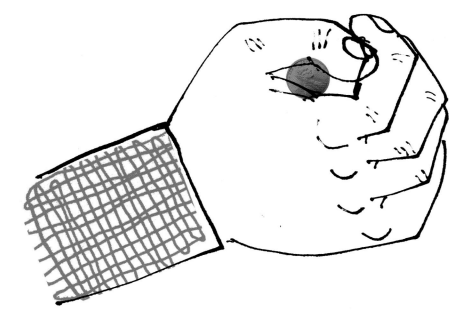

I'm off to my next adventure,
and I have no idea where I'll end up next.

Maybe I'll see you
sometime soon
in your town,

in your house,

your school,

your car,

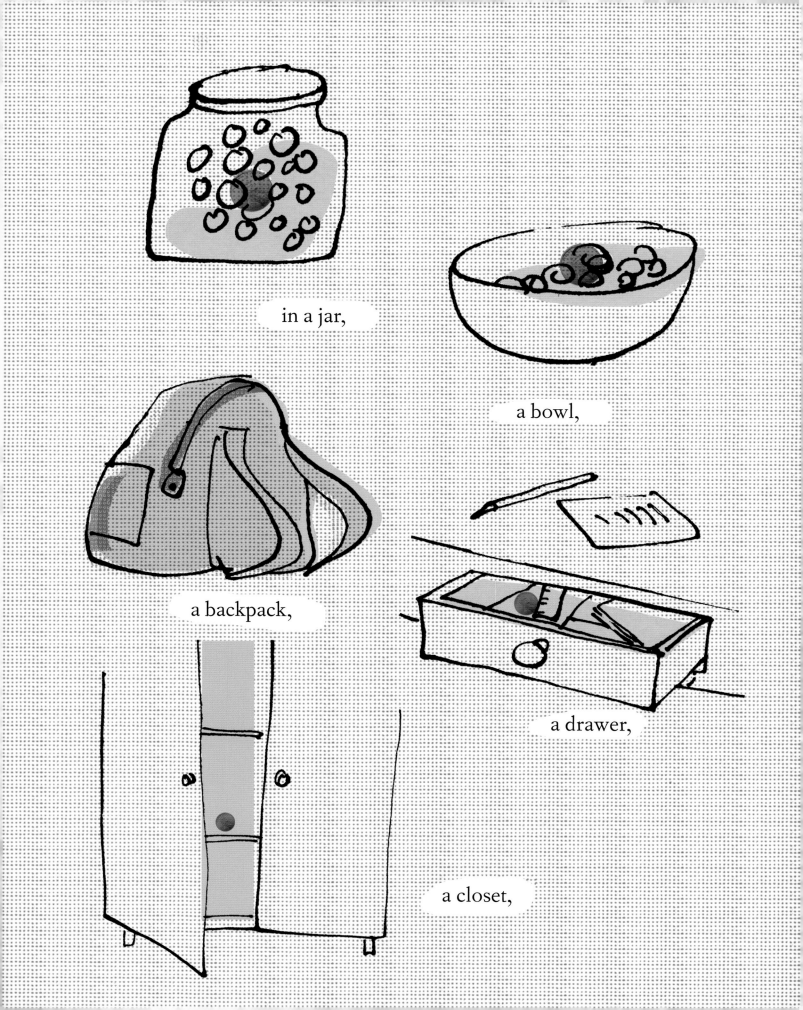

in a jar,

a bowl,

a backpack,

a drawer,

a closet,

or anyplace else that makes sense to find cents.

A Brief History of U.S. Coins

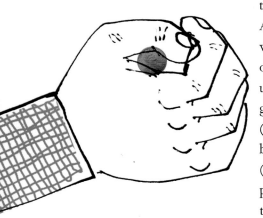

In the seventeenth century, the first European settlers in New England traded with Native Americans for furs, tobacco, lumber, and other things they could ship back to Europe and sell. Soon, coins from all over Europe found their way to the fast-growing American colonies, which were still part of Great Britain, to be used as payment for goods being shipped in (imports) and goods being shipped out (exports). At this time, people could pay for things in America with British money or other foreign coins including French louis, German thalers, Dutch ducats, and different Spanish silver and gold coins, including the Spanish milled dollar.

In 1783, the thirteen colonies defeated the British in the Revolutionary War, and then everything changed.

In 1784, a member of the Congress of the Confederation, the soon-to-be-famous Thomas Jefferson from Virginia, argued that the country needed its own system of money. Jefferson suggested that the money be based on a simple dollar unit built on a decimal system because "the most easy ratio of multiplication and division is that of ten."

After a few more years of debate, the new government, with George Washington as its president, decided in 1791 to create the United States Mint. It opened in 1792 in Philadelphia, which was our nation's original capital. The first coin minted was the "half disme," and later that year came the first cent, which looked nothing like the cent we know today. On its front was a lady with flowing hair, who stood for liberty. This one-cent coin was larger and made of 100 percent copper, compared to our current cent which is made of copper and zinc.

Back then, British money was still commonly used in the U.S. The British pound wasn't divided into 100 cents like our dollar, but its smallest coin was called a penny (or pence for plural), and that's how our one cent piece came to be known as a "penny." In the U.S., there are 100 pennies in a dollar and in Great Britain, since 1971, there are 100 pence in a pound.

Between 1792 and 1909, the penny had many different designs and sizes. There were large cents, half cents, Flying Eagle cents, Indian Head cents, and many others. In 1909, Victor D. Brenner designed the Lincoln cent we know today. From 1909 until 1958, the Lincoln cent had two pieces of wheat on its back, known as "Wheat Ears." In 1959, the Lincoln Memorial image replaced the wheat ears on the back of the penny. In 2009, the Mint celebrated the 200th anniversary of Abraham Lincoln's birth and the 100th anniversary of

the first Lincoln cent by making four different commemorative pennies. Since 2010, the backside of the penny has featured a new design with a union shield and the words ONE CENT in big letters.

So what's a penny worth these days? It depends on whom you ask. Critics claim pennies are worthless, a waste of the copper and zinc the U.S. government uses to manufacture them. Some groups are asking Congress to ban the penny outright and stop the U.S. Mint from making them. They say that pennies have outlived their usefulness since nothing costs a cent anymore, not even a piece of candy or a stick of gum. They point out that because each penny costs the U.S. Mint about two cents to make, this is not a good use of taxpayer dollars.

But many others disagree and think pennies are valuable, a part our American heritage, a rich reminder of our nation's history, a long tradition that should be honored and continued.

According to the U.S. Mint, pennies are the most widely used coin currently in circulation. In 2014, the Mint produced more than 13 billion coins, of which 8 billion were pennies. About half of these Lincoln cents were produced at the Philadelphia Mint while the rest were made at the Denver Mint.

Interesting Facts About Pennies

U.S. coins, including the penny, stay in circulation for twenty-five years on average compared to eighteen months for U.S. paper dollars, which are made by the government at the Bureau of Engraving and Printing in Washington, D.C., and Fort Worth, Texas.

If you stack sixteen pennies, your pile would be an inch tall. So it would take a pile of nearly 240 million pennies to reach from the earth to the moon (239,000 miles).

A rare 1943 copper penny that was made by mistake was sold to a coin collector for $1.7 million in 2010.

The Latin words *E Pluribus Unum* can be found on U.S. coins and dollars, including the penny. This phrase means "Out of many, one," and refers to how the original U.S. colonies came together, fought for independence from Great Britain, and founded the United States of America.

Additional Resources

usmint.gov/kids

usmint.gov/mint_programs/circulatingCoins/?action=
circPenny

treasury.gov/resource-center/faqs/Coins/Pages/default.aspx

Furgang, Kathy. *Everything Money: A Wealth of Facts, Photos, and Fun!* Washington D.C.: National Geographic Kids, 2013.

Reid, Margarette S., and True Kelley. *Lots and Lots of Coins*. New York: Puffin Books, 2011.

Yeoman, R. S. *A Guide Book of United States Coins*, ed. Kenneth Bressett. Whitman Publishing, 2015.

To lost pennies everywhere —R.S.

To Neal and Randy,
and to Marcelino, who picked up 273 pennies in one week in New York City —S.B.

Text copyright © 2017 by Randy Siegel

Illustrations copyright © 2017 by Serge Bloch

A Neal Porter Book

Published by Roaring Brook Press

Roaring Brook Press is a division of Holtzbrinck Publishing Holdings Limited Partnership

175 Fifth Avenue, New York, New York 10010

The art for this book was made with humor, pen, and digitally in Photoshop.

mackids.com

Library of Congress Cataloging-in-Publication Data

Names: Siegel, Randy, author. | Bloch, Serge, illustrator.

Title: One proud penny / Randy Siegel ; illustrator, Serge Bloch.

Description: New York : Roaring Brook Press, [2017] | "A Neal Porter Book." |

  Audience: Ages 4–8.

Identifiers: LCCN 2016025025 | ISBN 9781626722354 (hardcover)

Subjects: LCSH: Cent—Juvenile literature. | Money—United States—Juvenile

  literature.

Classification: LCC CJ1836 .S55 2017 | DDC 737.4973—dc23

LC record available at https://lccn.loc.gov/2016025025

Our books may be purchased in bulk for promotional, educational, or business use. Please
contact your local bookseller or the Macmillan Corporate and Premium Sales Department
at (800) 221-7945 ext. 5442 or by e-mail at MacmillanSpecialMarkets@macmillan.com.

First edition 2017

Book design by Jennifer Browne

Printed in China by RR Donnelley Asia Printing Solutions Ltd., Dongguan City, Guangdong Province

1 3 5 7 9 10 8 6 4 2